ERYRI

The Story of Snowdonia

by Michael Senior

© *Text: Michael Senior*

Copyright © by Gwasg Carreg Gwalch 1999

ISBN: 0-86381-549-9

Published in 1999 by Gwasg Carreg Gwalch
12 Iard yr Orsaf, Llanrwst, Wales LL26 0EH
☎ (01492) 642031
Printed and published in Wales

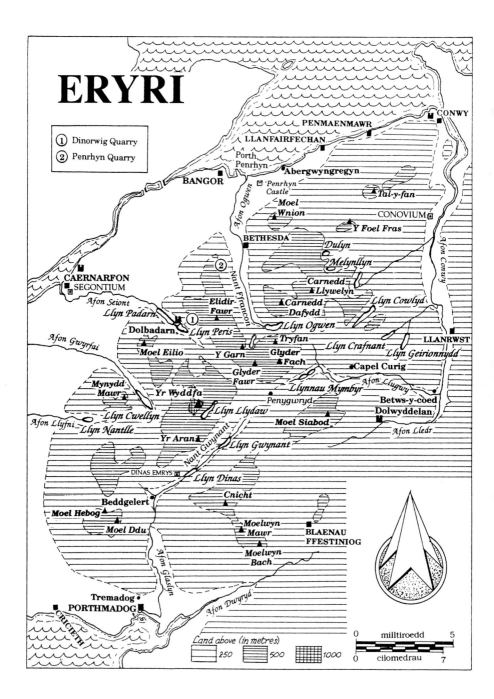

Contents

Introduction

I must not pass over in silence the mountains called by the Welsh Eryri, but by the English Snowdon, or Mountains of Snow, which gradually increasing from the land of the sons of Conan, and extending themselves northwards near Deganwy, seem to rear their lofty summits even to the clouds, when viewed from the opposite coast of Anglesey.

So Giraldus noted, on his journey through Wales in 1188. This proves the ancientness of both terms, but while it explains probably quite correctly the origins of the name 'Snowdon' (the 'don' part coming from the same Saxon word which gave us 'dune' and 'down'), it does not offer help with 'Eryri'. It was George Borrow who established the modern conventional wisdom: it was called Eryri 'by the Britons, because in the old time it abounded with eagles, Eryri in the ancient British language signifying an eyrie or breeding-place of eagles.' There is no doubt that the Welsh word for eagle is 'eryr'. Borrow hints in a footnote at something which has been more firmly established by Sir Ifor Williams, that there was a root word 'er' meaning 'to rise' from which both these words come: the rising place, and the rising bird. 'It is possible,' runs Borrow's footnote, 'that many will be disposed to maintain that in the case of Snowdon the word is intended to express a rugged excrescence or eruption on the surface of the earth.'

Pennant (who coined the name Snowdonia) disagrees. He thinks that the Welsh term means the same as the English, and that Creigiau'r Eryri, the Eagle Rocks, is simply a mistransliteration of 'Creigiau'r Eira', the snowy crags. His editor then confuses the whole thing further by saying that this seems to be a translation of Snowdon back into Welsh which was anyway a mistranslation in the first place, of Eryri, the eagle country, as 'eiry', snowy.

To Borrow Snowdon was 'no single hill' but a region. He does not use Pennant's term. Now the first name is normally used to refer to a single group of peaks, the second to the region as a whole, as in the Snowdonia National Park. This is the same region covered by the term, whatever its origins (though I personally am with Sir Ifor Williams), Eryri.

It is the upland zone. It is defined by contrast. Two valleys limit two of its flanks, to east and south in almost rectangular lines. It falls sharply to a coastal plain, and at one point to the sea itself, in the north; and in the west the Dwyfor valley separates it sharply from the Llŷn peninsula.

Pen yr Oleu Wen from Cwm Idwal

THE MAKING OF THE MOUNTAINS

THE geology of Snowdonia is immensely complex, one result of which is that any attempt to do it full justice immediately becomes tedious. There are so many qualifications which must be made and sub-divisions inserted. The great geologists who have written about this area, such as Greenly and North, struggle with the dilemma of trying to convey accurate information while telling an almost incredible tale. On the face of it, it is hard to make something so apocalyptic sound dull; yet science can find a way.

Here I want to sketch a kind of synopsis, which will, however, remain true to the underlying complexity, and which will, I hope, convey the salient points of the aeon-long saga.

What we see in Eryri is the residue of a largely destroyed landmass which was itself originally the reworked debris of an anciently vanished land. What we regard as high peaks today are the worn-away remnants of a much vaster smooth-sided shallow sloped dome. If this seems improbable enough it is outdone by the next point. The whole of this was laid down in the form of even layers of sediment under an anciently vanished sea.

So long ago that is would be futile to rehearse the millions there was another country here. In the course of enough time, and in conditions where rainfall is possible, everything in the end gets worn away. The pressure of one layer on another, and the sea above them, gradually formed the sediments into bands of rock. Two things then occurred to complicate the issue, both of them consisting of forms of pressure caused by the nature of the earth's core and crust. Molten matter forced its way through weaknesses in the strata, some of it remaining embedded in them, some bursting through to fall back onto the sea's floor. All this so far gave rise to horizontal even layers. It was another sort of pressure, this time coming from each side, which caused the layers to become buckled or folded, forcing the upper parts of the resulting undulation up out of the sea, where, incidentally, they could become eroded again by rain and return as sediment to take their part again in the age-long cycle.

In rough schematic form it goes like this. 1. Deposition. 2. Uplift. 3. Erosion. The erosion gives rise to deposition again and the whole thing

Clogwyn Du'r Arddu

Pre-Cambrian rocks: 'the Padarn ridge'

The higher peaks reveal the rhyolite,
an igneous rock, of which they are composed

starts again, repeated a presumably infinite number of times.

We see Eryri today in the middle of one of its phases of erosion. If we had been here some hundred million years ago we would have seen a vast high gently rising plateau. If we could wait long enough we would observe it all levelled off again, slipping finally into an all-embracing sea. Except that it would not of course be 'final'. In due course another Snowdonia would be thrust up and go through this whole process again.

In the meantime, since this is the time we happen to be here, let us take a closer look at the Eryri which we have, and consider exactly how it came to be the way it is. As far as the matter it is made of is concerned, there are some simple distinctions which may be made.

The mountains are made of two broad groups of rocks, the sedimentary rocks which are the deposits of the eroded older land, and the igneous rocks which have been blown out of the earth's core. The latter appear on the surface in two different ways, either having erupted there or having infiltrated the strata of sedimentary rock and been revealed by erosion. Rhyolite, the name of which comes from the Greek word 'to flow', is a common version of the first form, lava which has poured out and cooled fast. This forms the peaks of several of the higher mountains, characterised by their sharpness, such as Tryfan and Snowdon. The other type of igneous rock, which has cooled far below ground and so more slowly, is of a coarser texture in which crystals have had time to form, and which often also contains seams of minerals for the same reason. Parts of Crib Goch are of this form, and the bulk of Penmaenmawr and Foel Fras in the northern uplands.

The oldest rocks can be regarded as the base on which the mountains were built, and appear in our area mainly in a craggy ridge running south-west from near Bethesda across the bottom of Llyn Padarn. These are known as Pre-Cambrian, being older than the Cambrian series so named by Sedgwick, and are part of the original make-up of the earth. The enormous resistance of the Padarn ridge explains another feature of this immediate area, the incidence on either flank of the Elidirs of massive accumulations of slate.

Slate is squashed mud. It owes its fissile nature to the position of its particles relative to the line of pressure which compressed it, and also to the presence of thin layers of minerals within them. The great quarries of Bethesda and Llanberis owe their ultimate origins to the flow of lava and sediment from the Snowdon area pushing material ahead of it up against the immovable barrier of the Padarn ridge.

Rocks in the glacial valleys
have been smoothed on one side by the ice

The Nant Ffrancon pass shows the 'truncated spurs' cut off by the ice

THE MAKING OF THE MOUNTAINS

The geological periods during which the rocks developed which made the mountains are divided into three, in which there are many component phases. If we consider that the last of these, known as the Tertiary Era, was the shortest of the three we get some inkling of the time-scale involved. It lasted more than sixty million years. Compared to that everything that has happened since can be regarded as recent and relatively fast.

Starting about a million years ago this part of the world began to get significantly colder. Climate changes occur largely as a result of solar activity, though it is sometimes speculated that unexpectedly sudden change could be brought about by an asteroid impact, the dust-cloud from which could filter out the sun. The effect, in any case, is that when the climate cools the winter ice fails to melt during the summer, and gradually increases in thickness.

The form of the land, when it became covered in ice, was basically as it is now; the ice modified its details. It was because the valleys already existed that the glaciers slid down them, borne by gravity downwards. As they slid they scoured away the jutting spurs and smoothed the valley bottoms. A river valley has a V-shaped profile, a glacial valley is shaped like a U. Nant Ffrancon is, famously, the perfect example of a glacial valley.

The area in general is widely littered with the signs of the ice's presence, its retreat and its eventual melting. So plain is this to us today that it is odd to think that until the 1840's it was not recognised that we had undergone an ice age at all. F.J. North, in his section on geology in 'Snowdonia', quotes a note by Charles Darwin that is worth repeating. He and Adam Sedgwick had been in Cwm Idwal in 1831 looking for fossils. They examined all the rocks with extreme care, 'but neither of us saw a trace of the wonderful glacial phenomena all around us. We did not notice the plainly scored rocks, the perched boulders, the lateral and terminal moraines. Yet these phenomena are so conspicious that a house burnt down by fire did not tell its story more plainly than did this valley. If it had still been filled by a glacier the phenomena would have been less clear than they now are'.

Darwin was in Cwm Idwal again in 1842, by which time no doubt his eyes were opened. Indeed Cwm Idwal has much to teach us about the ice ages, in particular the fact that there was more than one. It has in fact no less than four terminal moraines, representing the stages of withdrawal of the ice, between which they show that there was temporary renewal.

A terminal moraine is the load of stones carried down by the glacier and deposited at its end, the point at which it stopped and then melted. We often see them, in fact, on our beaches. Up here in the hills they show us the extent of the late glaciers, as things began to warm up on the plains below.

Sharp ridges are one of the results of the eroding effect of the ice

*Mountain lakes show the shape of the glacial valleys,
as here at Padarn*

Their effect, by acting as a dam, is to give us mountain lakes. It is doubtful that without this, and the gouging out by the ice of rock basins, there would be any lakes in our area. The lakes are a glacial feature.

Lateral moraine is the burden of stones, fallen from the cliffs scraped and gnawed by the ice, which were deposited as it melted along its flanks. They can tell us the glaciers' thickness. We can also see their extent by the scratched and smoothed rocks which Darwin referred to, the side facing the oncoming ice being as if moulded, the side away from it often broken off and so sharp and jagged.

From these signs we can see that every valley had its glacier, the largest being in the Ogwen valley, where, in its upper stretches, it was over a thousand feet thick. A large glacier also filled the Llanberis valley, fed by two tributaries off Snowdon, from Cwm y Glas Mawr and Bach. Six glaciers ran off Snowdon altogether, two (from Cwm y Llan and Cwm Dyli) joining the Nant Gwynant glacier, and two going off on their own from Cwm Brwynog and Cwm Clogwyn.

The ice in the main valleys thus gained its mass and depth, and in the process its quarrying effect cut off the bottoms of the tributary glaciers to leave, now, 'hanging valleys'. When the ice fell back the last glaciers to linger caused the mountains to crumble back to the hardest rock of their makeup, leaving us with the cliffs at the back of Snowdonia's characteristic cwms, those small and deep lake-filled rock basins, carved by the last ice and damned by its moraine, which usually face north-east, where the ice could last longest. The effect of this eating back into the slopes also gives us another very characteristic feature, the sharp two-sloped ridge, or the strip of remaining rounded hill running between two steep slopes.

Darwin also mentions perched boulders, and these too form a distinguishing feature of the upland area. They stand in places to which they could not have fallen, often precariously perched as if about to tumble down the slope, thus proving that they have not rolled there either as any momentum would have carried them on. These have been simply dropped where they now are by the melting ice, having been carried on its surface (if they are sharp-edged) or if they are rounded in or underneath it.

The lakes themselves vary quite surprisingly in depth. The shallowest is Ogwen, which nowhere reaches more than ten feet. Eigiau and Idwal are surprisingly shallow too. The deepest is Cowlyd, which has been recorded at 222 feet, followed by Llydaw at 190, Dulyn 189 and Glaslyn at 127. In long historical terms all our lakes may be seen as being in the process of silting

Cwms, such as Idwal, formed where the last of the ice ate back into the mountain

The lake at the bottom of Nant Ffrancon is now silted up

THE MAKING OF THE MOUNTAINS

A large area of marsh at the head of Llyn Eigiau shows us this process taking place, the lake once having occupied all this area; and at Llyn Ogwen we can see a promontory forming from the silt carried down from the slopes of Glyder Fawr by the rushing stream which drains Cwm Bochlwyd. The lake which once undoubtedly lay at the bottom of Nant Ffrancon is now completely silted, and may be seen as a large basin of marshy ground.

Thus we can see, with our own eyes, that the landscape is in motion. The time-scale, measured against human lives, is immense, but one thing we can also see is that it is speeding up. When we dealt early in the chapter with geological time, the time it took for the rocks themselves to form, we were talking about hundreds of millions of years. When we came to glacial time we have to think only in tens of thousands. The greatest of the successive ice ages occurred some 18,000 years ago, the earliest about 26,000, and by 10,000 years ago the ice had gone. Since then the rivers have continued to carry silt towards the sea, gradually wearing away the mountains.

The speed of change has been increased, of course, by our own arrival. Clearing the uplands and then the valleys for agriculture we have encouraged the process of erosion, further increased by the denuding of the slopes by sheep. It is only vegetation which holds the soil in place, and where the sheep, over the last two centuries, have stripped it we can see the bones of the mountain becoming increasingly visible. With the top soil gone the vegetation cannot return, and erosion takes place so much the faster.

The Nant Ffrancon is a classic U-shaped glacial valley

UPLAND HABITATIONS

T the height of two thousand five hundred feet in the Carneddau lies a plateau of solid peat many feet thick. Analysis of the pollen found in such upland peat beds in this area has shown that the land at this height was once clothed in alder, birch and hazel. Today these would not grow much above eight hundred feet. They flourished at two thousand feet in the post-glacial period known as Boreal, from 7000 to 5500 B.C., when the climate was warm and fairly dry, and were succeeded in slightly wetter (but still warm) times by alder and oak, in a period known as Atlantic. This ended in about 2000 B.C., and before that time the only open ground in North Wales was along the coast, on exposed headlands where the forest was thinned by the salt wind.

This was the situation when human beings first penetrated our area. If you look at a map of neolithic structures, which started to be built here in about 2500 B.C., you will see that they strikingly cling to the coast. It is only in the drier weather of the Sub-Boreal period, from 2000 B.C. to about 700, that a difference in the climate began to thin the forest at its upper edges and made the establishment of flocks feasible.

Climate has always governed human settlement and activity, and if we think we are undergoing a climate change at present we should simply bear in mind that this is nothing new. There have been vast swings of change before. Human activity may accelerate a process which is taking place, and the introduction of flocks of sheep and goats during the Sub-Boreal period prevented the forest from recurring in the uplands just as in cooler and drier times the tree-line was declining. The population of the hills was thus enabled to expand.

Cairns and perhaps stone circles are products of the Bronze Age, and both may be found very widely scattered and in great numbers in the mountain area. The Bronze Age cairns may be found both on hill summits and on low and level ground, some, as that on the summit of Moel Hebog, at over 2000 feet, and those which form the summit cairns of Carnedd Dafydd, Carnedd Llewelyn and Foel Grach at over three. These are burial mounds. Where they have not been anciently robbed the occasional successful excavation has revealed a central cell containing a cremation in an urn. They do not indicate the existence of habitations at these considerable

Megaliths such as this in Bwlch y Ddeufaen
testify to prehistoric use of the uplands

The quarry has now destroyed the site
of a large stone age axe factory on Penmaenmawr

Stone circles such as 'The Druids' Circle'
above Penmaenmawr may belong to the Bronze Age

heights, and indeed none has been found. The location of the dwellings of the Bronze Age people is a continuing puzzle, since the frequency of their burial cairns and mounds, together with their very considerable activity at the copper mines of the Great Orme indicates that they must have been numerous. There is the possibility that a complex of hut circles and compounds in the valley below Llyn Dulyn, north-east of Carnedd Llywelyn, may be Bronze Age, but even if this were proved it would account for only a fraction of the population which must have lived in this area at that time.

Just as the Great Orme copper mines undoubtedly occupied many people during the Bronze Age, so at an even earlier point did the stone axe factory on Penmaenmawr, at the extreme north of the mountain area. This extended, at its peak, over a distance of two miles, and seems to have been in use for several hundred years. It is now, unfortunately, largely destroyed by the quarry, but was fairly thoroughly investigated before it went. Axes of several types were produced, for light local use and for export for forest clearance. Since they have been found as far away as Cornwall and Northern Ireland the enterprise, in about 2500 B.C., implies trade, as does the copper production some seven hundred years later, and trade in turn implies political organisation. It would clearly be wrong to underestimate our prehistoric predecessors.

The fact that we do not know where they lived may be due simply to the slightness of their dwellings, in a warm climate free, apparently, of the need for defensive structures. We know a little about their lives, however, from the things they made, some samples of their artefacts having been clearly identified. Some urns and a number of swords and daggers were found at Beddgelert, and a magnificent shield on the slopes of Moel Siabod.

If we know a great deal more about the people of the next phase of our history, the Iron Age, it is because they built substantial defensive citadels. We know from this at least that they had the need to, and so must envisage a society based on the idea of territory and hence both politically organised and settled. Once again we find their hillforts occurring mainly in connection with the coast, but here there are exceptions.

The first defences at Dinas Emrys, below the lakes in the Gwynant valley below Snowdon seem to have been from the first or second century, and there are signs of early Iron Age use. A defended hill also occurs at Dinas, further down that valley below Llyn Dinas, and in the same area there is a substantial small fort on Pen y Gaer, beside the Aberglaslyn pass. All of this indicates that the mountains were penetrated up this valley at an early period. Two other small forts occur at the edge of the upland area above the

Heaps of stones containing cremation urns are a Bronze Age feature

*Dinas Emrys shows signs of
having been defended in Iron Age Times*

coastal plain near where the river Dwyfor emerges from the hills at Dolbenmaen. And at Llanberis a small fort, now much damaged, occurs directly above the back of the town. Otherwise there is little to indicate that the hill-fort building tribes inhabited the upland area.

Things are very different when we consider the evidently more peaceable early remains. Huts and enclosures associated, in some cases, with field systems crowd the foothills and creep into the uplands, making it clear that by the time the Romans came (to which period some of them have been dated) the hills, except for the barest summits, were being fairly intensively farmed.

Since this form of dwelling, known as the round hut, was clearly in use over a considerable period we cannot allocate the remains in general to any particular phase. Rather we may say that it spans the whole of our early history, from the time of the coming of the Iron Age tribes in the first thousand years B.C., perhaps before that, through the Roman period (here in the hills probably largely undisturbed by that) and out again into the Dark Ages and early medieval times.

Sometimes the huts occur singly, sometimes in groups; sometimes the groups are within an enclosure, though this is evidently more an agricultural compound than a defensive work. Certainly they also occur within the hillforts, sometimes clearly contemporary with them, at others possibly indicating an afteruse of the ramparts for containing cattle rather than keeping out enemies. The actual form is a simple one, and easily recognised, since it is a ring of stones embedded in the earth. This formed the foundation of a wigwam-type construction made of birch or alder boughs and roofed with peat or thatch. Destructible but endlessly replaceable, the form is adaptable to either permanent settlement or seasonal migration.

The best examples in our area occur at high levels and so are rather inaccessible. This does not necessarily indicate a pattern of distribution, since any ancient structure would be vulnerable at lower levels to destruction by agriculture and in the building of walls; but the climatic factors we mentioned at the start of the chapter are relevant, since it was comfortable to live, and more convenient to farm, at heights of over a thousand feet in earlier times.

A NEW ORDER ARRIVES

I F you take the road across the neck of the Llŷn peninsula from Caernarfon to Porthmadog you will find that the familiar twisting Welsh lane becomes, either side of Dolbenmaen, startlingly straight. Experience leads me to suspect the imposition on our haphazard countryside of imperial order. Sure enough there was discovered, in the course of excavation of a gravel pit, a small Roman fort near to the site of the former railway station at Bryncir, a mile or so from Dolbenmaen. It had at least two barrack blocks, and was occupied during the first century A.D. Nothing of it now remains to be seen, but its existence marks the furthest west the Romans appear to have settled on the mainland in North Wales.

Since there must therefore have been a road at least from Segontium to Bryncir, we may suppose that it continued to Porthmadog and so formed an alternative route to the fort at Trawsfynydd to that normally assumed to run via Rhyd-ddu and Beddgelert. In any case the Roman occupation of North Wales marks out a sort of boundary to the area being dealt with in this book, penetrating it definitively at two points.

That the legions went through the mountains as well as round them is proved by the existence of a marching camp at Penygwryd, at the junction of the Llanberis and Nant Gwynant passes and on the route to Capel Curig and so a link, as we shall see, to the main north-south route. This indicates that the mountain passes were used as well by the Romans, which in turn suggests much more of a network of communications in North Wales than the evidence on the ground by itself has so far shown. Only traces of early, possibly Roman, roads have been found in the central uplands, one at Penygwryd in fact said to be later than the camp and lost, in any case, under the modern road.

It must be said as well that there is nothing to be seen in the way of Roman ruins at Penygwryd now. Only a possible indication of a wall in the form of a bank in the field running down to the road as it sets off down to Nant Gwynant may show the outline of the fort. The hotel lies on its northern border, and the whole embraces the road junction and the start of the two southerly forks. The east side of the fort is now submerged in the artificial lake.

The Roman road through the mountains at Bwlch y Ddeufaen
can often be seen in the form of a ditch

*The base of the Roman walls of Caer Llugwy
can be seen among the tree roots*

*An outline of the fort can be traced as mounds
in the field on the river bank and among the trees*

24

If a road ran to Caernarfon this way, it left the main Roman road in the area at Caer Llugwy, otherwise known as Bryn y Gefeiliau. Here, for once, there is something to see, in the form of recognisable banks in a field where the walls of the fort once stood. You can even see in places the stone bases of the walls.

The existence of Caer Llugwy had long been suspected, and could anyway have been inferred because (like the outpost at Dolbenmaen probably on one route from Caernarfon to Trawsfynydd) it lay at the right distance to be a posting-point from the fort in the Conwy valley, Canovium, now Caerhun. Ancient Roman ruins on the river Llugwy had been known about and then forgotten, but in the 1920's the site was properly excavated.

To find Caer Llugwy you take the old coaching road which deviates from the present A5 just as it crosses the Llugwy river, about half way from Betws-y-coed to Capel Curig. The fort lies between the road and the river, at a point where the latter does a big loop away from the road and back. This loop encloses the Roman fort. Its form is the usual rigid rectangle. Excavations have indicated that it was in use between 90 and 140 A.D.

The presence of Caer Llugwy at this particular spot tells us something about the route of the great Roman road known as Sarn Helen, which, it is known, ran from Canovium to Trawsfynydd and thence south to the main Roman town in Wales, Maridunum, now Carmarthen. A stretch of this is clearly identifiable in this area, where it runs across the uplands from the top of Betws-y-coed down to Pont-y-pant in the Lledr valley. This would lead us to expect that it followed the west bank of the Conwy valley until it met the Llugwy. The posting fort would then have been at Betws, and its presence a couple of miles upstream means that for a time at least there was another route taking higher ground from Canovium to drop to this point, then perhaps running downstream to the known part of Sarn Helen at Betws.

It hardly needs to be repeated that a main feature of the Roman military technique was this establishment of permanent lines of communication between the main occupied forts. In many parts of Britain these roads set the form of the future network, and are there still under our modern roads. In this area we are lucky to be able to see them in two instances unmodified, one being the stretch of Sarn Helen between Betws and Pont-y-pant already mentioned. The other is the connection from Canovium in the Conwy valley to Segontium at Caernarfon.

This runs across the hills between Tal y Fan and Drum, through a pass known as Bwlch y Ddeufaen, the pass of the two stones (after the magnificent standing stones which so clearly identify it) and falls to the coast

A marching-camp lay at the road junction at Penygwryd

at Aber. It is probably one of the first Roman routes to be established, since invasion of Anglesey was an early priority. It was, Tacitus tells us, 'feeding the national resistance'. Hence in 61 A.D. Suetonius Paulinus set out from a base in Chester to march through North Wales and conquer Anglesey. To do so he had to establish the fort on the crossing of the Conwy river, and from it this route across the hills. It was then used again in 77 by Agricola, on his more forceful and more successful expedition into North Wales, when the forts at either end of it took a more permanent form.

That we have even these two pieces of road is perhaps surprising, and the lack of more than fragments of the probable connecting roads may be explained. Substantial road building did not take place in Britain as a whole until the time of Hadrian, who came to Britain in 122 A.D. But at that time Roman interest in Wales decreased, as pressure increased in the north of Britain. With Wales for the time being reasonably settled the two main forts here had their garrisons severely cut at the time when manpower from all over Britain was concentrated on the building of Hadrian's wall, in the 120's. It thus seems likely that the road-building programme in North Wales was left unfinished, which is why only short stretches of the intermediate roads have been found.

We are able to put a date to the period when the roads were in use through the lucky discovery of fully datable Roman milestones. One, on the northern plain below the foothills lies on the evident route of the road from Canovium to Segontium, and dates from the time of the emperor Marcus Aurelius. Another on the same route but further west is from the time of Trajan. Above Llanfairfechan on the northern slopes, not one but two stones, found ten yards apart, marked presumably a revision in the route the road took coming down from Bwlch y Ddeufaen. These, found in 1833, are now in the British Museum. The earlier of the two records the eighth mile from Canovium and commemorates the year 121 A.D., that of Hadrian's visit to Britain. The second dates from between 207 and 209, the time of Septimus Severus.

Though other signs of the Roman presence have been found – such as a minor earthwork near the route of the road approaching Segontium, and a bath-house just west of Tremadog – there is nothing to see of them today, and the main impact of their occupation seems to have been confined to the network of roads and forts which they spread around the central mountain block. By simply marching through it they hardly affected it at all. The inhabitants continued to live independent lives in their round huts (there is no sign of the introduction of the square Roman form, or of the villa-

Part of the camp at Penygwryd lies under the artificial lake

*A mound on the slope running down to the road
may be all that can be seen of the Roman camp*

homestead with which more hospitable parts of Britain were dotted), and indeed one may speculate that if the Roman presence was noticeable to them at all it was as something of a convenience as a protection against other invaders and the source of a settled and stable way of life. Great military engagements meanwhile took place elsewhere. Here in the hills the absence of interference let a way of life continue which, with its associated culture, flowed naturally from the pre-Roman Iron Age to the post-Roman Dark Ages.

A square-built hut near the Roman road at Bwlch y Ddeufaen
may indicate Roman influence

REFUGE OF PRINCES

PARTLY because of its security, the heartland of North Wales has from time to time had a role to play in the country's history. Indeed if any particular spot could be regarded as central to Wales' identity, it must be Dinas Emrys. Because it lies at the foot of the Snowdon massif itself and overlooking the junction of the Nant Gwynant pass with the descent to the Aberglaslyn, Dinas Emrys is in a highly defined position geographically, and this is matched by its position in history and culture. There are signs (as mentioned in an earlier chapter) that it was in use from before Roman times and into them, and it was certainly occupied shortly after that; a substantial settlement had arisen there by the second half of the fifth century.

Dinas Emrys occurs in one of our earliest literary sources, the 'History of the British' by a Welsh priest called Nennius, who wrote about 800 A.D. Here (with some support from the Anglo-Saxon Chronicle) we can discern what actually happened in the sixth century. The king of Britain, named as Vortigern (which scholars now think was more of a title, 'High King', than a name) was in trouble with the Germanic tribes he had allowed to settle as mercenaries: in exchange for provisions they supported him against the Picts and the Irish, who were causing problems after the Roman withdrawal. The Germans brought their families over, and as their numbers increased he was unable to keep up the provisions. As they took control his advisers told him to withdraw to a fortifiable place. ' . . . and at last they came to the country called Gwynedd; and when he was exploring in the mountains of Eryri, that is, in English, Snowdon, he at length reached a place in one of the mountains that was suitable for building a stronghold'. Later in the story we hear how the hilltop came to be called after Emrys, the British form of the Roman name Ambrosius. The tale forms, in fact, something of a sequel to the story of Lludd and Llefelys in the Mabinogion, where it is said of the location of the events 'the form by which that place was known thereafter was Dinas Emrys'.

The web of story surrounding Dinas Emrys is complex, and in fact occupies a full chapter in my book 'Gods and Heroes in North Wales'. Vortigern, on arriving, failed to build his citadel, and was told by his wise men to sacrifice a child who had no father. Such a child was found, and turned out to be Ambrosius, in history the British leader who rallied

Dinas Emrys in the Gwynant valley is an important early site

A marshy hollow on the summit of Dinas Emrys
may be the site of the story of the dragons

resistance after Vortigern's failure. In the story he acts the role later filled by Merlin (a character adapted from this same story by Geoffrey of Monmouth), the prophet who foretells the future of Britain. He tells the wise men that there are dragons buried there (and the story of Lludd and Llefelys in fact tells us how this came about), and when this proved correct there occurs the famous image of the dragons fighting, the white (representing the Saxons) driving out the red, the British dragon, which, however, will eventually recover and win. The red dragon had been a particularly North Wales element since the seventh century, when it was the battle standard of King Cadwaladr; Henry Tudor, his remote descendant, flew it as his personal standard at the Battle of Bosworth. Meanwhile it had been adopted as the symbol of Wales as a whole, and when the Black Prince, as Prince of Wales, fought at the battle of Crecy he and his Welsh troops rallied to that banner. It is interesting, standing on Dinas Emrys today, to think that this is precisely the spot where the symbolism arose.

When Dr Savoury of the National Museum of Wales excavated this hilltop in the 1950's he found some evidence of the origins of the legend. There was an early-Roman-period man-made pool on the hill's summit, where the dragons were said to be buried; and over part of it was a Dark Age period paved platform. A flourishing community lived there in the time of Vortigern and Ambrosius, the mid fifth century. A later lord evidently took refuge there as well, since the only clear sign of occupation there now is the keep of a 13th century castle, about which nothing more is known. The hill is now in the hands of the National Trust.

Although (as the story recognises) most of the island of Britain became in due course occupied by Germanic tribes, the heartland into which Vortigern retreated and from which Ambrosius rallied remained independent and free long after the Anglo-Saxons themselves, in the rest of Britain, had become subject to the rule of the Norman French. Attempts by the Normans to complete their conquest by subduing Wales came up against the barrier of this inner heartland, which, not surprisingly, they failed to penetrate. There are thus Welsh castles here rather than Norman ones (and that on the summit of Dinas Emrys is likely to be such).

During this time of independence North Wales had a highly-structured political system, within which both artistic culture and religion flourished. The prince had a court in each district, and moved between them. At Dolbenmaen, for instance, there is a motte, now surrounded by ruined farm buildings and clothed in trees, which was once the castle from which the district of Eifionydd was ruled, which later moved down the river Dwyryd

*Dolbadarn Castle was the first of the independent
Welsh castles to feature a round tower*

*'Llywelyn's Cottage' may lie on the site
of the Prince's court at Beddgelert*

to Cricieth. Earth-work and timber castles such as this were superceded in the 13th century by stone-built structures, and a fine example of one of these stands beside the Padarn lake.

Dolbadarn Castle was built by Llywelyn the Great in the late 1220's or early 1230's, not at the site of one of his courts which controlled the 'commotes' or administrative districts, but rather on a line of travel between them. It defends the route through the hills via the Llanberis pass, just as Llywelyn's other main castle at Dolwyddelan controlled another traverse of the mountains through the Lledr valley. Although Llywelyn had done much to unify Wales, and was a force to be reckoned with by the English crown, the presence of these castles reminds us that his position was never secure. The stronger the Welsh princes were, the more they were surrounded by the resentment of the displaced. Indeed Dolbadarn castle is famous for having been (according to Leland, in the 16th century), the place of imprisonment for some twenty-two years of Owain, the defeated brother of Llywelyn ap Gruffudd, who, like his grandfather Llywelyn the Great, had fought his nearest relatives to gain the princedom.

Dolbadarn Castle is unusual for its time in having a round rather than a square tower. This was a new form which was being developed by the Normans along the border at this period, but had not before (as we may see at Dolwyddelan) been used in Wales. Llywelyn worked towards this more effective form of defence with D-shaped towers at Cricieth, Ewloe and Castell y Bere. Dolbadarn is unusual too for having three floors, rather than the usual two.

The keep which you see at the moment is only the best remaining part of a more extensive defensive layout. Closer inspection will show the hill on which it stands to have been surrounded by a curtain wall (once some ten feet high, now reduced to less than three), within which once stood a hall, a tower to the west, another building on the eastern side, all grouped around a courtyard.

Llywelyn almost certainly had a court at Beddgelert, where the story of the faithful hound (an international popular tale with no special Welsh connection) became attached to his name. 'Gelert's grave' is now perhaps the little town's best-known feature, but is of course entirely spurious. The name Beddgelert does in fact mean the burial place of Gelert, but he was the founding saint of the parish, not a dog. The story of the hound was introduced by the landlord of the Goat Hotel, a Mr David Pritchard, towards the end of the eighteenth century. He it was also who provided the village with the grave, an enterprising piece of tourism management which has certainly paid off. It makes the point that people greatly prefer fiction to fact.

A mound shows the site of a motte-and-bayley castle at Aber

*Pen y Bryn is a strong contender for the location
of Llywelyn's court at Aber*

'Llywelyn's cottage' is a late 17th century building, but may of course stand on the site of his court. There is a monastic connection which makes it seem likely that he would reside here when in this area, since the surrounding land had been granted by him to the Abbey of Aberconwy in about 1200, to which he had given its original charter and where he also had a residence. Llywelyn's keen interest in monastic foundations is amply proved, and this area would have appealed to him since there was a priory here from very early times. Indeed it was said (in 1286) to be the oldest monastery in Wales after Bardsey, its venerable status being due to its position on a route from England to Ireland. The probability is that the original foundation dates from the sixth century, although of course there are no remains earlier than the twelvth or thirteenth centuries, when buildings started to be constructed in stone. It was at this time that Giraldus described it, saying it was an independent order but coming under pressure from the Cistercians of Aberconwy. It did not, however, become a Cistercian monastery, but shortly after Giraldus' time adopted the Augustinian rule. It is probably to this period that the earliest features of the present building belong.

The present parish church of St Mary is all that is left of the ancient priory, the lancet window at the east end and the fine Gothic arches of the north transept dating from perhaps 1230, and along with some possibly older stonework of the north wall to the west of the transept letting us feel the atmosphere which surrounded the Augustinian monks. It is, Pennant remarks in the 18th century, a situation which is 'the fittest in the world to inspire religious meditation, amidst lofty mountains, wood, and murmuring streams'.

Giraldus and his colleagues were travelling through North Wales raising support for the Third Crusade, in the company of Archbishop Baldwin. Having skirted the south of the mountains they went on past Caernarfon to Bangor, where there was also (by 1188) an ancient religious foundation. Indeed it is probably true that St Deiniol founded the first monastery here in the sixth century. It enters history in the Irish annals, where it is said to have been sacked (presumably by the Irish) in 634. The 'Chronicle of the Princes', the Welsh annals, records that it was sacked by Vikings in 1073. By the time of the Norman invasion of Wales it had become associated with the cathedral, but in Llywelyn's day it was still a scattering of dwellings, which, it seems likely from some foundations below the college building, may have occupied the site of the present university. The marshy hollow at the foot of the college grounds is thought to be the possible site of the holy well. A number of burials were also found nearby. This in itself would seem to indicate that the settlement here predates the building of the cathedral, the earliest form of which belongs to the early twelfth century.

Foundations of that early church have been discovered, but all that remains of it above ground is a fragment of its apse in the south wall of the recent structure; this takes the form of a blocked-up round-arched window and a protruding piece of buttress. The original church here was burnt by King John, together with the town and probably the ancient monastery, on the second of his two invasions of North Wales in the year 1211. The bishop's support of Llywelyn nearly cost him his life. He was arrested in his church, but ransomed himself for the price of two hundred falcons.

This penetration of John's men so far into his inner territory, and the destruction of the important spiritual centre, was too much for Llywelyn. He succumbed to the pressure of his advisers and sued for peace. The treaty was humiliating, and he paid heavily both in fines and loss of territory. What had happened was that King John had avoided the usual mistake of invaders of coming from Chester to Deganwy, and by approaching instead from Oswestry had avoided the problem of the Conwy crossing and so penetrated the heartland itself. Usually the Princes could feel safe in this natural citadel, protected from Chester-based invaders by the defensive barrier of the Conwy river. Edward I at a later date was to use the same strategy, penetrating the inner sanctuary by taking Llywelyn's castle at Dolwyddelan, and then encircling the mountainous heartland itself.

It was because it was normally impossible for enemies to cross the Conwy, with the Welsh defending its western bank, that Llywelyn and his descendant Llywelyn ap Gruffudd were able to have one of their main courts at Aber, on the northern coast. It might be worth noting here that whenever the place is named in the Welsh chronicles the name of it is 'Aber': 'bu varw Dam Siwan, verch Ieuan vrenhin . . . yn llys Aber', and so on. Our historic sources, Leland, Pennant, Byng, Fenton, all knew it by that name. In modern times the historians Bezant Lowe, the compilers of the Royal Commission on Ancient Monuments Inventory, Professor Dodd, H.R. Davies and John Davies all call it Aber. Whatever justification there may be for the recent imposition of the name Abergwyngregyn, there is none in the historical sources.

The Chronicles note that Llywelyn's beloved wife Joan, daughter of King John, died at his court at Aber; and later that his son Dafydd died there too. Since it was also the place from which his successor Llywelyn ap Gruffudd negotiated with Edward I we might be justified in supposing that this, among all the courts of the independent princes, was one of the most important.

The location of Llywelyn's court at Aber is a matter of dispute. It is often supposed, following Leland, that the motte known as Pèn y Mwd forms the site, since he says some of the building still stood there in his time. Pen y Mwd is a round twenty-two foot high earthwork close to the river. In style it is recognisable as the motte of a Norman motte-and-bailey castle, with no sign of the bailey, and so would have been likely to be of the period immediately preceding Llywelyn's castle building. It must be said firstly that the sites of Llywelyn's courts (as opposed to his castles) are often not known, an argument for supposing that they did not normally involve mottes; and that this is confirmed in the two cases where sites of his courts have been identified and thoroughly investigated, at Llanfaes and at Rhosyr in Anglesey. These lead us to suppose that somewhere under the turf of Aber there are stone foundations of substantial buildings.

Such apparently do lie under the drive and yard of Pen y Bryn, a house dating from about 1600, in its present form, which stands on a brow overlooking both the site of the motte and the coastal plain. In its position if nothing else Pen y Bryn proclaims itself to be an anciently settled site. The route of the Roman road in its descent apparently loops below it, where banks and ditches clearly form the outline of a defended position. Much old structure still stands on the site, including a barn with massive stonework and slit windows which are, it is said, the oldest in Wales. The more extensive works which once stood there are outlined under the ground, but it must be said that they might equally well be farm buildings of a later period as Llywelyn's court. Until further work is done and datable material discovered the matter remains open. Nobody who has stood on this spot, however, and looked out over the Lafan sands and the crossing to Llanfaes could not be tempted to believe that this was the site of the family court of the princes, where both Llywelyn's wife and son died.

SLATE AND STONE

SLATE has been used as a building material at least from Roman times. It was in use in the Middle Ages and roofs began to be commonly made of it during the sixteenth century. Of course it was more commonly used, both by the Romans and the Norman castle-builders, in areas where it was plentifully available. We hear of it early in North Wales. As early as the fourteenth century slate was exported from here to roof Chester castle. In the time of Elizabeth I there was a healthy export trade to Ireland, single slates selling at 1/8d per thousand, doubles at 2/8d. Some three to four hundred thousand slates were sold to Ireland in the ten years after 1583.

The word comes from the Old French 'escalate', as also does the English word 'slat', meaning a splinter, something fractured or split. As was explained in an earlier chapter it gets its fissile property from the parallel arrangement of its particules, itself the result of the mode of its formation, by extreme pressure from one direction. Its abundance in the area of the lower Ogwen and Peris valleys has had a profound effect on the region.

The trade with Ireland which started so early became, in the eighteenth century, the underpinning of the future industry. From about 1721 trade to the continent of Europe reinforced this. In the 1730's Caernarfon was exporting around two million slates a year.

This was not then an organised business. From the early 1700's the Vaynol estate, which owned the area of the parishes of Llanberis and Llanddeiniolen, in which the most accessible slate lay, had absent owners. Sporadic private quarrying at this time allowed a large number of individual shallow quarries to develop on the east bank of Llyn Peris. Increasing demand towards the middle of the century led to the merging of these into partnerships. By 1772 there were five such partnerships in operation above Padarn and Peris.

Penrhyn at that time also had an absent owner. The Williams family had remained in occupation until 1684, but in the early eighteenth century the estate became split between two co-heirs, one of whom lived in Devon and London, the other in Cheshire. In 1765, however, the Williams heiress married John Pennant, a rich sugar planter returned from the West Indies, a man from the same ancient Flintshire family as the writer and traveller Thomas Pennant. He at once started to buy out his wife's co-owner's interest in the Penrhyn estate, and then to let off leases to quarry in the area

This view published in the Illustrated London News
in 1858 shows the scale of the Penrhyn quarry

The quarry town of Bethesda takes its name from the chapel
founded there by early quarry workers

The owners of the Dinorwig quarries
built the port called after it 'Port Dinorwig'

around what is now Bethesda. This set a pattern which was to be repeated for the rest of that century: Penrhyn and Vaynol alternated in innovation, but each carefully watched the other's moves.

When Thomas Pennant made his journey through North Wales in 1773 the slate industry was already a prominent part of the economy. 'The quarries are becoming now the source of a prodigious commerce', he says, annually exporting 'many millions of slates.' Lord Penrhyn 'has added greatly to the population of the country by the improvements he has made in the slate business.' The passage, however, owes not a little to hindsight, and must have been a revision from a later phase of his tours, since John Pennant was succeeded by his son Richard in 1781, and the latter did not become the first Baron Penrhyn (an Irish peerage) until 1783.

It is true that it was due to him that the slate business flourished. Unlike his father, who simply let the quarries, he took the whole lot in hand, systematically buying out the leases and not renewing them as they expired, until he could manage the business as a single unit. This was the start of the Penrhyn quarries at Bethesda. From about 1780 onwards the effects of the Industrial Revolution on the construction industry accelerated, as the introduction of steam power led to a concentration of the workforce around purpose-built factories, and hence the building of many uniform terraced dwellings. For these (and indeed the factories themselves) a seemingly insatiable demand for standard-sized roofing slates had come about.

Vaynol, meanwhile, the estate which owned the other side of the Elider mountains and hence the western end of that mass of slate, had been taken over in 1787 by a consortium of businessmen, who rented the quarrying areas on a twenty-one year lease from its absent owner and thus founded the Dinorwic Slate Company. By 1791 this was exporting from Caernarfon some two and a half million slates a year.

Vaynol, in fact, controlled Caernarfon as a port, obliging the Penrhyn slates to leave from the river mouth known as Aber Cegin, where, in 1790, Lord Penrhyn built a port. Pennant tells us that in 1792 'upwards of twelve thousand tons were exported' from there. Porth Penrhyn was a busy place, always thronged with vessels. From there, says Pennant, 'the slates are sent to Leverpool, and up the Mersey by means of the canal to all the internal parts of the kingdom, and to Hull; from whence is a second exportation: numbers are shipped for Ireland, for Flanders, and even the West Indies.' He also mentions that the production of writing slates was a Penrhyn speciality.

Transport, of course, was always a problem to the slate industry. A

*'Vivian's quarry' near the Welsh Slate Centre
shows the solid slate make-up of the mountains*

*The workshops of the Dinorwig quarry
are now the interpretive centre of the industry's history*

tramway ran from Penrhyn quarries to Porth Penrhyn from 1801. In this Vaynol lagged a little behind. It was not until 1824 that a tramway connected the Dinorwig quarries with the then new port of Port Dinorwig.

The outbreak of war with France in 1793 put a sharp break on the construction business and halved the exports from Port Penrhyn. A war tax on slates of 20 per cent and upwards penalised the coastal trade. Business recovered with the Peace of Amiens in 1801, and a few years later the Battle of Trafalgar made the seas safer for shipping. By 1809 Port Penrhyn was shipping slates to Boston, Massachusetts.

All this of course had an immense effect on this remote and unpropitious area. In the first forty years of the last century the populations of the quarrying areas doubled and in some areas trebled. New towns came into existence around the slate terraces. In 1820 a group of Non-Conformists, themselves mainly quarrymen, built themselves a chapel near their new working quarters and called it, after the biblical pool with healing waters, Bethesda. The rise of Welsh Non-Conformism at this time gives a strangely biblical look to the map of North Wales, since the habit was to name the new Independent chapels after Old or New Testament places or characters: Ebenezer, Carmel, Bethel, Saron, Nebo. Pubs, cottages and more chapels quickly followed these remote foundations. By 1865, with a population of five to six thousand, Bethesda was four times that of the whole of its parish in 1801.

Another feature which was partly spurred by the expansion of the industry was the improvement of the roads. When Pennant first visited Nant Ffrancon he descended into it by 'a most dreadful horse path . . . worked in the rudest manner into steps'. Some twenty years later he reports that 'a noble coach road is made, even beyond Nant Ffrancon'. This was Lord Penrhyn's work, and it set the future pattern of communications. When Telford was commissioned, in 1817, to route the London to Ireland road through North Wales, he used Lord Penrhyn's stretch of coach road, and hence the new main road ran, conveniently, right past Penrhyn quarries. Road building, at that time, was seen partly as a form of poor relief, since the ending of the war had led to a slump and widespread poverty.

As both construction and industry picked up again after the war the slate business boomed again, profits of around £7,000 in 1820 increasing to £30,000 in the 1850's and more than £90,000 by 1861. All was not however by any means harmonious. Right from the start the industry had been run on a system of bargaining between quarrymen and owners, and given the hard conditions and the power possessed by the workforce in a demand-led market it was not long before industrial unrest became

Visitors can still see the craft of slate-work being practised

systematic. A strike at Penrhyn in 1825 shocked the whole industry, and was settled with the remedy of some grievances. By 1874 the workers were better organised, and able to deal with the owners on more equal terms. This however was not a situation which the Penrhyn family intended to continue. A lock-out in 1896 was evidently effective, since this response was tried again in 1900. The famous three year lock-out which then followed probably had a decisive effect on the future of the slate industry as a whole. Although of course it enabled the Dinorwig quarries to boom, without Penrhyn in operation the national supply of slates was unable to meet demand, with the result of the commodity becoming overpriced in relation to competing materials. With a change in tastes and house-styles in the new century slate roofs were seen, in the new suburbias, as urban and old-fashioned, so that those who could have afforded what had now become something of a luxury no longer wanted it, and in spite of a revival in the late 1940's to serve the post-war rebuilding programme the industry never again reached the heights it had achieved in the mid-nineteenth century.

When the Dinorwig Quarry closed in 1969 its substantial repair and maintenance workshops were abandoned but left standing. Being so solidly built they have remained much as they were, and now house 'The Welsh Slate Centre', a working museum, part of the Padarn Country Park. This complex in general forms a tourist facility of the highest quality, and gives a useful insight into the industrial history of the mountains. Indeed with the pumped-storage power station almost alongside, occupying the base of the closed quarries, it is clear that the industrial use of Snowdonia's natural assets still goes on.

The Slate Centre still has much working machinery, and displays the quality and surprising versatility of slate. It is worth a visit if only to experience a sense of the astonishing power of its gigantic water wheel. This giant, the largest in mainland Britain, was erected in 1870, worked until 1925, and is now restored to running order. Fifty feet in diameter, it produces eighty horse-power and runs all the wheels and cogs of the foundry and all the workshops, this free power for ever being created simply by the weight of the water which falls gently into the giant wheel's buckets. It rumbles with the hum of serious business, the implication of power. In a world in which much is often fake it shocks you to come up against something so real. This is serious. This is no toy.

The makeup of the mountains has proved to be an aspect of their destiny, and certainly the slate business has left indelible scars. The stone of which they are made has also, like the slate, affected their use and so their

*Mr Gladstone's visits when Prime Minister
made the quarry town of Penmaenmawr a fashionable resort*

*Penrhyn Castle is one of the most impressive
legacies of the slate industry*

appearance. When the demand for slate dropped off that for stone, largely used in road building, carried on, with the result that Penmaenmawr, on the north coast, is a fraction of the mountain it once was.

Penmaenmawr mountain started to be worked in the late 1820's, its stone having been recognised since prehistoric times as of special durability. Not strictly granite, though always referred to as such, this particular type of pyroxene granophyre owes its hardness to the uniform distribution of its crystals. By the 1870's 'Pen' was producing sixty to seventy thousand tons of stone a year. By 1905 it had ten miles of tramway, and the stone was being used in sixteen British counties for the building of roads. In 1911 the merger of two companies increased the quarry's efficiency, and its success continued with the accelerating road programme. In the 1960's a deal with a German company led to direct shipments to Hamburg, for the building of German roads. The western Hamburg by-pass, for instance, is made out of Penmaenmawr mountain. So, with the increase in its stone's use in concrete, are the walls of the Mersey tunnel, the air-strip at Bristol, and New Brighton's swimming pool.

While this industrial use was taking away the mountain, Penmaenmawr enjoyed a contrasting success as a resort. In 1895 a guide book to North Wales described it as a 'pleasant watering place' and 'one of the most enjoyable of the many resorts which have sprung up during the last half century along the coast of North Wales'. This was of course the result of the coming of the railway, in the 1840's. The station opened in 1860, and already in the 1860's the town was advertising 'bathing boxes' for its visitors. Its neighbour, Llanfairfechan, followed suit. But Penmaenmawr had an asset, in the competition for fashion, which Llanfairfechan lacked. It had Mr Gladstone.

William Ewart Gladstone first came to Penmaenmawr in 1855, when he was Chancellor of the Exchequer. He came by train for a three week holiday from his family home of Hawarden Castle, on the Welsh border. He came for the sea bathing, and to work, at the time writing his study of Homer. Then, and during the eleven further visits he made over the following forty years, he stayed in rented houses, mostly owned by the Darbyshire family, the quarry-owners. When he became Prime Minister in 1868 this seal of approval made Penmaenmawr smart and fashionable. 'I do not know of a more healthy place, and a more satisfactory climate is not to be found, to my knowledge, in this country,' said the great man. Today we may wonder at the need for such heights of oratory to describe so drab a place, but the sad fact is that Penmaenmawr's fall during the second half of this century was as dramatic as was its rise during the second half of the last. Now at last, as I write in the late 1990's, something is being done about this, and 'Pen' may eventually again retrieve its pride and elegance.

One other legacy of the quarrying of the mountains is the great estates of the quarry-owners with their country houses. Even the lesser quarries, such as the one called after its owners, the Oakley family, north of Maentwrog, which survived in use until 1971, produced the fine seat, Plas Tan y Bwlch, which is now a study centre run by the National Park Authority. At Vaynol, on the Menai Strait, the Assheton-Smith family, when they eventually came back to North Wales to run their quarries, built alongside the original Elizabethan mansion a fine country house which perhaps incorporates a smaller early eighteenth century one. There is no doubt that one of the most striking and historically complex developments arising out of the value of slate was the succession of events at Penrhyn.

The descendants of Ednyfed Fychan, the lieutenant of Llywelyn the Great, possessed a large amount of land in the later middle ages, and one of the most notable of them, Gwilym ap Gruffudd, built himself a house at Penrhyn in the early fifteenth century. He expanded his lands by purchase until the estate covered almost the whole of the parish of Llandegai. The family took the surname Griffith, when Henry VIII recommended that the Welsh gentry adopt hereditary names and the Acts of incorporation of England and Wales encouraged this. Gwilym's descendants also owned the Cochwillan estate (where the house, a fifteenth century hall, has been recently restored to habitable use), and confusingly adapted the first of his names rather than the second and called themselves Williams.

Griffiths resided at Penrhyn until the sixteenth century, when it was bought by their cousin John Williams of Cochwillan. Williams was an ecclesiastic who was already, and was to become more so, prominent in British politics. He was made Lord Keeper of the Privy Seal in 1621, and bought Penrhyn in 1622. He went on to become Archbishop of York, and played a significant part in the Civil War.

The estate, as we have seen earlier in this chapter, became eventually split, and was restored to unity by the Pennant family, who both bought and married into it. Richard Pennant in 1785 bought out the remaining shares. When in 1808 he died childless his widow remained there for some years, but the property had been left to a cousin, George Dawkins, who, between 1821 and 1835, built the castle.

If this grotesque monument to pretension seems laughable to us now, we have to remember the late 18th century taste for the Gothic and the

Picturesque. It was not until just after the Napoleonic wars that circumstances combined to enable the building of follies on a truly vast scale. The ending of the war left the country poor, unemployment out of control and starvation a constant threat for many. At the same time it revitalised the construction industry, and hence the market for slate and stone.

It remains a choice as to whether one describes the building of these massive structures, and the great walls around the parks of estates such as this and that of Vaynol, as a form of 'poor relief'; or as the exploitation of fortuitously cheap labour. The two are different facets of the same thing, the choice of phrase a statement of one's point of view rather than historical fact. Gwrych Castle near Abergele is a good example of this scale of landscape decoration by a quarry-owner, and being finished in about 1816 it may well have influenced Dawkins. He commissioned the architect Thomas Hopper, who had done some work for the Prince of Wales, to design and supervise the work.

The Pennant family lived in Penrhyn for at least some of the time from its completion until 1949. (Dawkins had taken the name on his inheritance, which now, by subsequent marriage, has become Douglas-Pennant). In 1951 the Castle, together with a large area of upland farms, was donated in lieu of death duties to the Inland Revenue, and the whole of this handed over to the National Trust. The Castle, which had been open to the public sporadically from the start, is now a popular tourist attraction.

Cochwillan now restored, was one of the original seats of the Williams family who bought Penrhyn from their cousins

MEN AND MOUNTAINS

L ORD Lyttleton, in the middle of the eighteenth century, referred to them as 'the formidable mountains of Snowdon'. He saw them as 'black and naked rocks, which seem to be piled one above the other; the summits of some of them are covered with clouds, and cannot be ascended'.

To all the early travellers Snowdon was a fearful place, and best avoided. Giraldus, in the twelfth century, had been awed by the sight of the mountains from Anglesey; Leland in the sixteenth said they were 'Horrible with the sighte of bare stones'. Camden, his contemporary, called them the British Alps, and said they were snow-covered all year round. The first people actually to approach them, apart from local shepherds, were intrepid botanists, such as the Reverend Bingley, who, in pursuit of rare plants, actually climed Clogwyn Du'r Arddu, in 1798. It is perhaps Thomas Pennant, who may be called the first tourist, who first paid attention to the mountains for their own sake, climbing Snowdon by the miners' track. It was largely Wordsworth who brought the romantic view of nature and Britain's wilder places to the popular imagination. Writing about the turn of the century he set the last part of 'The Prelude' on Snowdon itself, where he describes a summer night-time climb to see the dawn. The grandeur of the mountain in the moonlight moved him to thoughts of God and infinity. The romantic age had arrived.

Once the fashion started artists and romantic writers flocked to the mountains. We shall see in the next chapter how the formation of an artists' colony is at the basis of the history of Betws-y-coed. The penetration of observers into the heart of the mountains was accelerated, from the early years of the century, by Lord Penrhyn's new turnpike. This ran from Capel Curig to the coast from 1802, and Lord Penrhyn added an inn to it, now Plas y Brenin, to which the various travellers came. A further road ran down the Llanberis Pass from 1830, and connected the Capel Curig turnpike with Beddgelert, where there were further hostelries, already, now the Saracen's Head and the Goat.

We get our clearest insight into the mountain area of the nineteenth century from George Borrow, who came up the Capel Curig road on foot in the 1850's. He dined at the Royal Hotel, as it became, where he felt

The ascent of Snowdon has been popular since the very start of tourism

The Penygwryd hotel formed the focal point of the start of mountaineering

Lord Penrhyn's inn on the new turnpike
became the Royal Hotel, now Plas y Brenin

conspicuous in his walking clothes 'amidst a great deal of fashionable company'. When he later climbed Snowdon he was not alone either: 'We were far from being the only visitors to the hill this day; groups of people, or single individuals, might be seen going up or descending the path as far as the eye could reach'. This familiar scene to us now was even then not new. In 1831 a visitor had recorded: 'There is no place more public than the higher ground of Eryri during the summer'. It was remarked in 1857 that 'Snowdon is ascended by everyone because it is the highest top . . . ' The path, Borrow remarks, was surprisingly good. The place had, it is clear, already begun to turn into a country park. A photograph of the summit in the 1870's shows a shanty town of shacks crowded with people and horses.

Some time around the middle of that century attention began to shift from the achievement of reaching the summit to the challenge of doing so by harder means. The walker came up the prepared track from Llanberis. The mountaineer saw Snowdon from its sharper side.

Already by the 1840's the farmhouse at Penygwryd had begun to double as an inn. In 1847 it was bought by a young farmer, Harry Owen, who ran it as a hostelry with his wife for the next forty-four years. Charles Kingsley depicts it in his novel 'Two Years Ago' published in 1857. Going in, you found 'a low room ceiled with dark beams, from which hung bacon and fishing-rods, harness and drying stockings, and all the miscellanea of a fishing inn kept by a farmer, and beneath it the usual happy, hearty, honest group'. Such was the success of this that in 1859 the inn was largely reconstructed. Kingsley himself came mainly for the fishing, but the inn was at the time frequented by famous Alpine climbers. The Climbers Club was in due course founded there, towards the turn of the century. But by then Mr and Mrs Owen had died, and with their going a change of fashion took place. The state of Penygwryd having deteriorated, its place in the climbing world was usurped by the inn founded by the 'younger' or 'new' Owens at Pen-y-pass. This became the centre of activity from 1900.

It was a literary and academic crowd, and in those years before the Great War seems to have had its own inbuilt nostalgia. It was a hearty and healthy scene, ' . . . with Frank Smythe, perhaps, crooning on his mouth-organ, perched in a bath towel on the back of the bench; Tony Smyth, the notable airman, and Humphrey Trevelyan, now the Ambassador to Egypt, or O'Brien and Longland, in abstract argument, through the steam; and George Mallory or young George Trevelyan leaping to do slow circles over the roof-beam . . . ' So Geoffrey Winthrop Young recalls, with unmistakable regret, the lost innocence of those days at Pen-y-pass 'before the war'.

The Great War changed the face of climbing as it changed so much else. Winthrop Young, writing (as above) in 'Snowdon Biography', in the 1950's, puts it thus: 'The war came; and it eliminated much of the more leisured class, and destroyed the balance between work and cultivated leisure'. It was, in fact, partly a social change. But with the sudden increase in accessibility which came with common car ownership in the 20's and 30's came also a change in attitude to the mountains. It was now no longer a question of coming in a group for some weeks during university vacations. Snowdon could be reached at the weekend from the midlands or Merseyside. This affected (as Winthrop Young puts it) 'the social elements from which climbers were drawn'. It also meant something more serious for the future of the sport. The focus before the war had always been on climbing mountains. Now it became (with more frequent attempts now possible on the same routes) a matter of climbing rocks.

Cliffs, such as Clogwyn Du'r Arddu or Lliwedd, had been used as practice grounds for some time, but always on the understanding that the techniques learnt were for the purpose of ascending peaks. Suddenly in the 1920's that outlook changed. Geoffrey Sutton, writing in the same invaluable book, identifies the moment as 'Fred Pigott's ascent of the East Buttress of Clogwyn Du'r Arddu in 1927'. Certainly the names of Pigott, Frank Smythe and Morley Wood are essential to the annals of the origins of rock-climbing. With the change in emphasis, and the change in the social class of those now enjoying the mountains, came a shift away from the hotels, as Young again says, 'in their happy solitude at the remote end of long walks and slow cart-drives' towards 'the coming of the hostel, the climbing hut, and the camp'. With this change in the 1920's yet another could be seen to be on the way.

When the focus moved from the mountain to the rock it soon led to attention to technique; and this in turn raised the question of the permissible limit of aids such as tools and mechanisms. When Morley Wood carried some stones up the Clogwyn in his pocket to jam into cracks, he opened up a vast debate. It was decided at the time that a stone native to the cliff might be restored, but not a foreign one introduced. Young comments: ' . . . we may now see the jammed stone as the thin end of a prodigious wedge, embodying an alteration not natural to the mountain and predicating immediately the metal peg, the hammer, and the pulley'.

Thus yet again a new era of climbing is born, and after the second world war it boomed again. Rock-climbers, like everyone else, seem to grow younger. Colin Kirkus was nineteen when he developed new routes on the

Clogwyn and on Tryfan; Joe Brown was twenty when he revolutionised the routes on the Clogwyn in the summer of 1951. By then Chris Briggs was at the Penygwryd, where in the early 50's the British Everest team were to make their base for training, and a new awareness of the mountains arose among the writers and broadcasters who might be found there.

All this is satisfactorily recorded in 'Snowdon Biography', itself a sequel, as it makes clear, to Carr and Lister's magisterial 'The Mountains of Snowdonia'. For a personal insight into what it was actually like to live there nothing could improve on Thomas Firbank's 'I Bought a Mountain', recently re-issued, in which by a magical facility of style Firbank evokes the hill country in all its moods.

The toll-house on the turnpike road

57

THE ADVENT OF TOURISM

We saw in the last chapter that when people started to come to visit North Wales they did so, at first, for a particular purpose; as botanists, for the purpose of scientific research; as mountaineers, later as rock-climbers. The high rainfall of the area gives the plentiful run-off required to form trout streams, and people came as anglers too, fishing its streams, rivers and lakes. Those who were also writers spread news of the area's beauty, which gradually enticed others to come just to view its landscape. It was only really when fashionable society could see this landscape itself, for instance hanging on the walls of the Royal Academy in London, that the habit developed of making the journey just for the sake of being there.

Improved roads facilitated this. For a long time the network of narrow drovers' roads, which connected the areas of upland pasture to the market towns, and the long-neglected Roman roads were all we had, and this combination kept the area isolated. In the eighteenth century through routes became developed with the formation of turnpike trusts (by which a commercial body was granted a lease, usually of twenty-one years, on a stretch of road, empowered to levy tolls in recompense for maintaining the carriageway). It was perhaps the formation of the Capel Curig Turnpike Trust in 1802 which started the trend to increasing accessibility which still continues. This linked to Lord Penrhyn's road from the coast to Capel Curig, and for the first time provided a serviceable through route through the mountains.

By 1808 the Shrewsbury to Holyhead mail-coach was using this. The importance of the route through Wales had increased greatly with the Act of Union with Ireland, which came into effect in 1801, and by the second decade of that century the turnpike system was beginning to look inadequate. Thomas Telford was commissioned to survey the roads through North Wales in 1811, and between 1815 and 1819 he rebuilt the road which is now the A5, in the process absorbing into his new route the Capel Curig turnpike. This involved the building of the Waterloo Bridge at Betws, which was opened in 1816.

Meanwhile the artists had begun to make North Wales' scenery famous. The distinguished art historian Peter Lord has written the definitive history of 'The Betws-y-coed Artists' Colony' (published by the National Library of

Thomas Creswick's etching shows the village
of Betws-y-coed as the artists first found it

The artists made the Royal Oak their headquarters

Other old inns in the Beddgelert area served visitors from the south

Wales), from which it is clear that the movement largely stems from the enthusiasm for the area of the highly regarded Royal Academician David Cox. Cox was a watercolour painter, who used the medium to convey an immediate response to what he saw before him, as he painted, in all weathers, in the open air.

Lord makes it clear that although Cox was not the first artist to paint in the Betws area, the fact that he made his base there drew others to do likewise. Before that artists had painted the area while passing through it. In the 1770's Moses Griffiths had depicted the area as the illustrator of Pennant's 'Tours'. Also in the 1770's Paul Sandby was one of the first to depict, in watercolour, the North Wales mountain scenery. Turner came in 1798, again travelling through; he came again in 1802, on which occasion he painted his famous view of Dolbadarn Castle. Cox himself had visited in 1805 and 6, and in 1836 contributed to Thomas Roscoe's book of engravings of North Wales. Roscoe stayed at the Royal Oak in Betws, and this may have influenced Cox's decision to make that inn his base when he came to stay in 1844, then aged sixty-one, and every year from then.

The Royal Oak thus became the centre of the artists' colony, which rapidly grew around Cox. It was a much simpler building then, having been several times rebuilt, 'a short, dark passage' (writes the contemporary William Hall) leading to 'the parlour, reserved for the company of "the higher order" . . . Bacon and hams hung from the kitchen ceiling . . . '

Betws was a quiet place when Cox discovered it, two or three inns and one small shop, beautifully depicted in Thomas Creswick's engraving of 1836. A few years after he made it his base it was described as overflowing with artists. You met them round every bend, on their way to or from their sketching grounds, their white tents and umbrellas 'to be seen in whichever direction the eye turned, suggested to the visitor the encampment of an invading army'. So again remarks Hall.

It is clear from their work that the artists were attracted by exactly the same things as are the tourists today. They painted Pont y Pair, the seventeenth century bridge which carried the old Llanrwst road across the river Llugwy. They painted the Swallow Falls, of course. They went up to Capel Curig to paint the three peaks of Snowdon.

When in 1868 the Conwy valley branch-line reached as far as this, business in Betws, now no longer reliant on the mail-coach, started the boom which has never really paused. The only fear now is that it will throttle itself with its own success.

The coming of the railway opened up Snowdon summit to the masses

Snowdonia's serenity survives its popularity

Tourism approached as well from the other direction, and early in the century the old inns of Beddgelert were becoming substantial hotels. With the opening of the Snowdon Mountain Railway in 1896 the sanctuary of the numinous mountain was finally breached. We have to be thankful that it is only in the summer that the summit becomes so congested with people who quite clearly could not have walked there.

Very many people, however, do; and this causes an increasing problem. Snowdon suffers worst, of course, because Snowdon is and always has been where everybody wants to be. The erosion of the paths by the sheer number of boots has led to a wholesale paving programme which has reduced much of the mountain to the character of a municipal park. The alternative, which no-one would recommend, is to be seen now even on the less popular peaks: the white scar of ever-widening track, as water erodes the top soil of trodden turf and walkers use the sides of the slippery shaly wound and so inadvertently make it larger. Since limiting visitor numbers would seem distasteful also there appears to be no solution apart from continuous, and one hopes sensitive, cosmetic treatment.

Cars too harm the scenery by their sheer numbers during the summer months. No-one knows exactly how many people come to Eryri, but a survey done in 1994 by the National Park Authority estimated that it had 6.6 million visitor days devoted to it per year. This represents undoubtedly a lot of people. Those not constrained by the bounds of school holidays can still catch the magic of which Wordsworth said

> . . . it appeared to me the type
> Of a majestic intellect, its acts
> And its possession, what it has and craves,
> What in itself it is, and would become.
> There I beheld the emblem of a mind
> That feeds upon infinity, that broods
> Over the dark abyss.

'THE STORY OF ...' Series

Wendy Hughes interweaves history, tales and events with attractive and interesting locations that will captivate and excite the visitor, leaving the reader breathless and surprised as she turns back the tide of time and glimpses into each century.

The Story of Gower. 88 pp; ISBN 0-86381-217-1; £3.75
The Story of Pembrokeshire. 100 pp; ISBN 0-86381-253-8; £3.75
The Story of Brecknock. 104 pp; ISBN 0-86381-316-X; £4.25

Radnorshire – A Historical Guide

– Donald Gregory. Radnorshire in many respects is Wales in a microcosm – hilly, wild, beautiful and small with the past ever present.
168 pp; 0-86381-284-8; £4.50

THE MICHAEL SENIOR SERIES – *A widely published historian with a series of well written volumes about different areas of North Wales.*

The Conwy Valley – Its Long History. 48 pp; ISBN 0-86381-035-7; £1.50
Llandudno's Story. 32 pp; ISBN 0-86381-391-7; £1.75
Anglesey – The Island's History. 64 pp; ISBN 0-86381-389-5; £2.75
Conwy – The Town's Story. 32 pp; ISBN 0-86381-345-3; £1.95
Caernarfon – The Town's Story. 32 pp; ISBN 0-86381-346-1; £1.95
Llŷn – The Peninsula's Story. 48 pp; full of illustrations; ISBN 0-86381-443-3; £1.95
Meirionnydd's Story. 64 pp; full of illustrations; ISBN 0-86381-442-5; £1.95

The Crossing of the Conwy

– Michael Senior. From prehistoric times to the new tunnel.
112 pp; ISBN 0-86381-191-4; £3.75

North Wales in the Making

– Michael Senior. A guide to the area's early history. Hard-back.
128 pp; ISBN 0-86381-322-4; £9.75

Two Bridges over Menai

– Robin Richards. History of the construction of the bridges across the Menai Straits. ISBN 0-86381-387-9; £2.75

This Valley was ours

– Eileen M. Webb. History of Nant Gwrtheyrn as remembered by one of the village's children. ISBN 0-86381- 428-X; £7.50